DANIELE BERGAMINI

Chants for Love

ISBN-13: 979-12-200-2055-8

Project, texts, illustrations and cover art by
Daniele Bergamini

This book uses the free font
EB Garamond

DEDICATION

Oh, my beloved!

This is for you,
for when you had words
like a generous mirror
I looked into
and glimpsed
a better myself
than that
I sometimes believe in

CONTENTS

(QUESTION AND ANSWER) PREFACE

Q: How was this book born?
A: A couple years ago I landed on Instagram to advertise a project of mine, two lines of apparel I designed with graphics and words.
Once there, I ended up stumbling on, and getting in touch with, a whole community of writers, poetesses and poets (mostly from India and Pakistan) very active in Instagram.
Before you ask: yes, they write on pictures (or, eventually, in the relative captions) and... just so you know it, I do it as well.

Because, after such contacts, I discovered in myself a poetic vein that I had never really explored (before, I used to consider myself more of a writer, or, marginally, a song-writer).

In the beginning of 2017 I had one of my many ideas: I wondered whether I could have written a series of poems, like poets of a remote past might have done, about love.
I tried with one, I tried with a second one... and in 52 days I ended up writing 100 of them!

Q: What inspired you, especially?
A: I especially found myself inspired by an arabesque imagination.
I like to fantasize about the chance that these chants were found in a library, perhaps collected in what claims to be the copy of a copy of a copy of an ancient manuscript... or, maybe, even that manuscript itself, directly found in an archaeological site, while digging the ruins of an old palace, and, somehow, preserved by the fading touch of time.

Q: Who wrote, who composed these chants?
A: I did it, of course. But, in the context I imagined, anyone.
You will notice a variety of nuances.
Most of these poems are simple, not looking after sophisticated words or metaphors.
In some of them I do it (within my limits, of course; in better hands, the same ideas would have blossomed much better...), yet lightly and rarely.
There is, I hope, something for everyone.

Q: For whom are these?
A: I intentionally kept a format in first singular person, dedicated to a second singular person.
And, excepted for a few cases, these can be dedicated by everyone, to everyone.
Personally... many of these reflect my situation, of someone who is waiting for love to come...

I. Wait

*"But, what if you came, and left
after finding my door closed?
When are you coming?"*

Chant no. 2 "Your blessed name"

Destiny plays cruel tricks
on my inconsolable mind,
by concealing from my knowledge
the melody of your name

Day and night
I call
each and every graceful and enchanting
thing, bird, flower, place, star, angel and virtue
known to man,
in any tongue born from Babel

And while I call,
night and day,
my palm lies on my heart,
the only one I can trust
will make me know,
for sure, 
with a rumble 
like tumultuous thunder, 
which one is your blessed name

Chant no. 61 "How should that be?"

When I tell them
for how long
I have been waiting for you,
they all give me advices
to help me to recognize you

A child with too much dirt on his face,
and too little food in belly, says,
"Must hug you, feed you, and promise
to never leave you in the street,
with nothing but your shadow,
turning into a monster every night,
to keep you company"

A pretty girl, with big jewels at her earlobes, whispers,
"Must be beautiful, and kind,
and treat you as if you were
the only light in the life"

An old woman, skin as wrinkled as rock,
charged of memories,
light of hopes, suggests,
"Must be strong, and well rooted:
a tree must bear fruit, for to be abated not"

A luminous angel came down from the sky
and proclaimed,
"God asks: - Tell me, how should that be? -"
I answered,
"I just hope, about myself, to be
whom my love may want
and seek"

***Chant no. 103 "The right time"**

Any time can be the right one,
for you, to finally come

Yet, it has not come, yet

I am still waiting for you,
with my eyes staring,
stubborn, indiscreet,
at the shifting shadows

And I wonder:
if the moment just gone
was not propitious,
is it mine, perhaps, the blame?

What should I do?

What if staring and waiting,
holding my breath,
was irritating it,

Like an insecure magician,
who cannot perform his trick
as long as you keep staring
at his shaking hands?

Chant no. 83 "Many, short waits"

I wait for the Moon the whole day,
pretending the Sun blinds my eyes

Then I wait for the Sun,
fearing things lurking in the darkness

I wait for the rain to wash me,
when my face is encrusted with mud

But I soon wait for its end,
otherwise new mud will not stick

I wait for lunch,
then I cannot even stand the sight of the food

I crave silence,
then I long for someone to talk to

I fill my life
with many, short waits
for to distract myself
from that of your coming,
apparently taking forever...
not never, I hope... true?

Chant no. 65 "Right into my lap (Their promise)"

I foolishly smelt
every bush of roses, irises and lilacs,
but I never recognized you

Yet, at times, I did not even dare,
fearing the bees and the wasps

I spied dim constellations,
with tools I could not figure out,
their ambiguous tongue divining
both victory and defeat,
and I, pompously smiling at the battle,
always returned crawling, aching

I looked into psalms and hymns,
and read, into the stroll of a mountain,
the way to what I wanted, but then,
I, like a slave wearing the king's crown,
forgot the gratitude
towards Who, solely, can move the hearts

They heard howling, me,
thirty and three thousand names
down dried pits, into abandoned shells,
but now I am left with nothing more
than a sore throat and inflamed eyes

They say I should cease,
for once,
to want and wait for you,
and to dig paths
with my worn-out shoes

Right then
- it is their promise -
you would fall
right into my lap!

But, what if, that day,
I, with my heart all withered,
walked away
without turning back?

Chant no. 54 "Directions"

I scrutinize ahead, frowning,
in the foggy crystal ball
of an enigmatic soothsayer,
but the blurred shadow I see
could belong to anyone

I gawk on my left,
among the crowd, scattered,
flowing everywhere:
if you were among them,
how could I ever recognize you?

I stare at the arduous path behind:
were we any close, perhaps, for once,
but I was looking elsewhere,
or, even though I found you, I let you go,
not recognizing you?

I glimpse on my right,
at the tombstones of my illusions,
each one nurturing a flower
bringing bitter pollen, and
lessons in their elliptic parlance

I look at the ground
and I wonder
whether I should renounce
to this moribund hope,
and bury it,
like you cut down and burn a tree
that grows and grows,
but never bears fruit

I contemplate the abysses above,
whose extents I cannot imagine
without faltering:
why does it seem easier
to find you in those feeble fires,
rather than on this ball of matter
we roam?

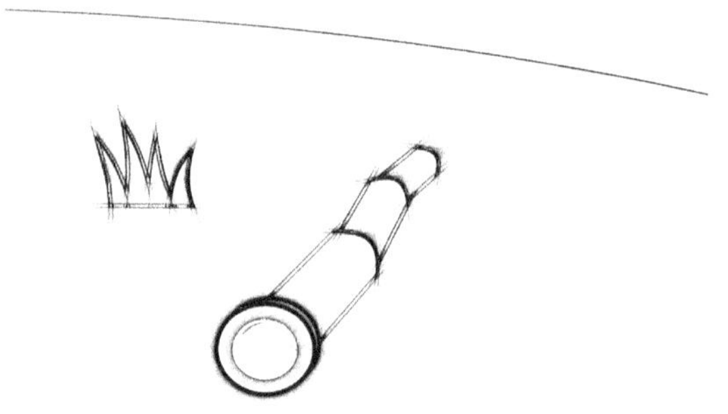

Chant no. 68 "It ended before"

There is no alley, no doorstep, no courtyard
that I have not dusted
with the echoes of my laments

How can I keep my calmness,
when I have lost your message?

I do not belong to the dead!

I looked under, above, behind and inside
every furniture, dress and thing

Under every tile

Am I this fool,
to lose your letter in my own home?

They asked me who sent it

Disconsolate,
I had to admit
that I do not know

The dream ended
before your name
could be
revealed

Chant no. 81 "The visit"

The way your lips and your tongue,
soft, moist, unquenchable,
get captured and abducted,
in a relentless and furious clutch with mine,
that no one wants either to win or to lose

The way your flesh fills
the cups of my palms,
offering itself
beneath your euphoric command
to these crazed hands
exploring the meanders
of your multitudinous treasure,
like a beggar
too swiftly turned
into a king

The way your whispers
torment my ears, my head, my guts, my marrow,
my very own cognizance of myself,
depicting me unearthly,
so marvellously that
when you cease,
to signify you mean them,
I implore you, in tears,
to tell me more

Then you say other words,
yet disgraceful, rough,
your voice
gotten as unpleasant
as grinding

Why?!
What happens?!
Who are you, truly?!

My eyes, incredulous,
open
on my solitude

I find my lips preserving
the flavour of piquant dishes

I find my hands ransacking
the wool of an empty, coarse cover

I find my ears hurt
by the hubbub down in the street
and by that insolent screech

I bite my own hands!
I howl!

Would you return to visit me,
if I fell asleep again?

Chant no. 78 "Desert wind"

Love is like a desert wind

Now it throws scatterings of sand
against your face,
to blind you and make you weep

Now it brings you faded petals, from far away,
to promise you a lush garden
it cannot let you find

Now it gathers mountains in the sky
pouring oceans on you, and now
it wipes them away, as if it was nothing

Now it drags you with itself, far from the ground,
as if angels were carrying you, and now
it slams you into the sand as if to bury you

And now it brings me a chant
Is it you? Should I follow its charm
and search for you in the wilderness?

***Chant no. 119 "My heart swears"**

My heart swears
you must be out there,
somewhere

And I, like an obeying slave,
like a zealous disciple,

I have been looking under the mountains
and beyond the stars and the worlds far away,
but I have not been able to find you

Oh, the glacial frown of my heart,
when it was accusing me
to have not looked enough
and to have not prayed enough

And it was and still is like falling
and never hitting the bottom,
and like being persecuted
by a fate making fun of me

Every single time

Now my heart has started saying
that it cannot exclude
it might have been wrong,
all this time

It looks at my wounds
and laments over them

Chant no. 28 "They stare at me"

I turn and turn
like a spinning top
when you dance around me
chaining my eyes to yours

And I laugh and laugh
and I reply with enjoyment
to your clever jokes

And I moan with pleasure
when your fingers fumble my hair
and you nibble at my earlobes
and you whisper to me your desire

(In my imagination)

They stare at me

With fear

Am

I

Falling

Into

Madness?

*Chant no. 109 "Autumn plea"

The Sun never ceases
his majestic run in the sky,
and the marching shadows
elongate and shorten
from our feet,
to remind us
of the unavoidable fall
hanging from our days

I see my youth
slip away,
like from a tree
surrendering
to the humbling Autumn

But there will not be
another Spring, for me,
after the Winter I already feel
biting and chewing
in my bones

I shake, more than if
I was covered with snow,
at the idea that you
are not here,
not yet

I do not even know your name,
yet my tongue
stumbles on every word,
doubting it may lead me
to savour
the way the world salutes you

I do not even know your face,
the colour of your eyes,
and then, I explore the rainbow,
wondering whether
it may have hints for me

Are you even destined to come?

Or, perhaps, was,
this life of daydreams I lived,
a mirage I fooled myself with?

Oh, it would be so terrible,
if you were not meant to happen!

It would be so tragic,
if this hope I have been nurturing
as if my very own life depended on it
was meant to die!

Because I painted all my days
with colours now faded and chipped,
only to find my present
oppressed by the darkness...

...please, come to me, finally,
and show me that
I did not waste my life
with the wrong dream!

Chant no. 29 "I stay at the door"

I stay at the door,
open,
day and night,
Spring and Autumn,
Summer and Winter,
staring at the street
sneaking in among the houses,
waiting for you

They come and feed me
and wash my face, hands and feet
and implore me to go back in,
sleep and take care of myself,
for the love of God!

But, what if you came,
and left,
after finding my door closed?

When are you coming?

II. Sparkle

*"What kind of malady
has been besieging me?!
What have you done,
to this soul?!"*

***Chant no. 101 "In the secret of my heart"**

What kind of malady
has been besieging me?!

My face suddenly burns,
my forehead drips

My hands engage in
a furious fratricidal fight,
whose point of contention
is absolutely unknown

My feet become dancers,
one exuberant step forward,
and two timid ones back,

Or they get forgetful,
as they often lead me
at your door, no matter which was
my destination

My memory is getting lost,
like ruins buried in the sand,
as your name, strangely,
replaces way too many words
in my speech

Or is my tongue hooked on it?
How can they say they understand me?

The heart gets indecisive
between pushing its way
out of my ribcage
and letting itself sink

Is, maybe, my soul, trying
to part from me?
how could I explain,
otherwise, all these sighs?

Why do I always wish
you were around,
for to tell you this, or that,

But when you are here,
I always forget
what they both were about?

I cannot sleep

I despise the time
passed in your absence

What have you done, to this soul?!

Oh, sweet conviction!
It can't be helped!
From now on,
in the secret of my heart,
I'll invoke you like this:
"Oh, my beloved!"

III. Dream and hope

*“Please, are you on your path
to me?”*

***Chant no. 108 "There's a room"**

Oh, my beloved!

There's a room
I have been preparing all this time,
ready to host you

On the door, built from my reception of you,
there's a nice plaque, smelt from my devotion,
with your name written in gorgeous handwriting
with the ink of appreciation

Inside, the wallpaper
is adorned with a pattern I hope you may like,
but if I had misunderstood your tastes,
or if you changed your mind, any time,
please, let me know,
and I will change it, accordingly to your heart

And the walls are decorated with paintings
depicting memories, places and people,
and there are empty frames,
and what is needed to paint,
to let you be creative with the shape of your dreams
and feel them real
as much as possible

The floor is covered with exquisite carpets
to protect your dear feet
from the cold or any harm,
and to let you sit or lie,
or even roll around, giggling,
like children do

The furniture,
that I build, repair and renew
all the time,
from my commitment,
is conceived to serve you as good as possible,
full of drawers with keys
to let you keep your sacrosanct secrets

But then, there's a key,
smelt from the freedom you will always have,
whose key wards are shaped
like the secret code
of my love for you

Would you accept it?
And... would you let me in,
one fine day?

That room,
you have to know,
is in my heart

Chant no. 33 "The olive tree"

Oh, my beloved!

I hide behind this old olive tree,
when, with the ones you hold dear,
you, immersed in a perfumed cloud
it is said could turn a lion into a lamb,
you, adorned, crowned with your hair,
interwoven with the matter of the Universe,
you, leave your home

And I do not dare to manifest myself
before your ardent coal eyes
and to talk to you!

Alas!
Too little, I know, of you!

I spend hours asking questions,
one for each leaf, to this tree
that knows you well

If only I had roots, bark, leaves!

Would you rest in my shade?

Chant no. 9 "Your eyes, in which I gladly fall"

Oh, my beloved!

Your feet are refined masterpieces,
and the ground raises up to meet them
and even the desert grows grass
so that they may not be scorched

Your sacred temple, lies,
guarded and revered,
waiting for whom
you will regard
as the elected worshipper

Your breasts are turgid fruits,
overflowing nectars,
picked in a forbidden valley
in a summer of daydreams

Your heart provides the rhythm
to which seasons
willingly subjugate themselves

If it ever ceased to beat,
under ice, the earth,
would be forever buried

Your smile is like the pardon
reaching the convicted,
right before the wretched executioner
gains his piece of bread

Your voice resounds in minds
as if it announced joy and abundance
and those who ear it
suddenly feel
enlivened in their courage

Your words sound, to the ear,
like that perfect epic
poets have been searching forever,
never finding it

Your eyes are deep pits
in which I gladly fall
and I do not want to be rescued,
for there I find what I had lost

But where are, you, my beloved?

Chant no. 86 "Scribe"

Oh, my beloved!

They whisper at my window,
when the shadows fall
to favour their allies,
and beg me to let them in,

and, once inside,
with their hands tormenting each other,
like ever-discordant twins,
they pour on me, like crumbling dams,
the weighing mass
drowning their hearts
from within

They implore me to pen, on their behalf,
the indescribable,
or even the indefinable,
about those who reside in their heart,
and to their heart give life,
by residing in there

I tell them no one may know
those feelings,
and their aim,
better than they do,
but they have already decided that
only I could find those words,
and they will not listen to reason

Under the light of an ardent flame,
letters and words blossom
on an untouched page,
at the pace of their blushed accounts
and of what I infer,

all this,
while I wonder
whether and where could exist
someone able to make poetry out
of all the indescribable and indefinable
your residency in my heart
creates

Chant no. 80 "I wish"

Oh, my beloved!

I wish I knew all the words
written in those books lying on dusty shelves,
to understand and express
all the ways my love for you takes

Would you know, yourself, their meaning?

I wish I could imagine new routes
(and I wish I had the courage to travel them),
to discover lands by now forgotten,
or where no one has ever set foot,
and name them after you

Would you leave, yourself, to visit them?

I have no glorious feats
you may admire
and be proud of

I have no prodigious qualities
to make me stand out
above any other

We are simple people,
after all

Would, a life-long devotion, my own, suffice?
I wish…

Chant no. 56 "Every artist needs a muse"

Oh, my beloved!

When I cook the food
for the people of this town,
I dream of you!
After all, every artist needs a muse!

I think of you
when you bite your lip,
and my pastries drown in honey!
Now people are euphoric!
This dance will wear them!

I dream of you,
and of your sinuosities,
while I stir my eggs
Some people told me
that my radishes pie
bit their nose!

I crave your smile, and you,
whispering my name,
while I am making a sorbet
So I mix up the vinegar and the rose water!
People roar like mad cats!

Oh, my beloved!
They have banished me
from that stinky kitchen!
I have got nothing else to do, except
devour spicy food
and pretend it is your love!

Chant no. 39 "The most daring, the least courageous"

Oh, my beloved!

I am like a burglar,
the most daring amongst all

As I steal,

like aquilegias in a flowerbed,
smelled and caressed,
and, nevertheless,
not plucked,

moments,
transfigured by your radiance,
I thirstily get inebriated with,
and my soul feasts upon,

whenever, unseen,
I admire you
and I lose myself in you

And I am like a pretender, too,
but the least courageous amongst all

*Chant no. 115 "Rain (Thirst)"

Oh, my beloved!

My heart jumps in my throat
and the blood in my head furiously flows as to break my veins
and my eyes avidly drink what they see, to get inebriated of it,
When you!
Like a furious leviathan assaulting the life out of the sea!
Like a graceful eagle taking the sky!
Like a powerful ram breaking down the gate of my composure!
When you emerge, joyful, radiant, magnificent, sublime!,
from the cobalt water of the pond that, for a short while,
was womb to your glorious body

And you walk on its shore, smiling,
and your beloved feet step on emerald grass and bushes of ferns

And I admire generous armies of drops of water
sliding, stopping, slowing down, accelerating,
on your ambrosially perfect shapes,
falling from your silk skin,
and I so wish I could lie before you, with my mouth open,
and drink that rain that your skin just scented!
But! I! cannot!

Then you shake your head, and spurts of water fly everywhere
And one reaches my cheek!
Alas!
I cannot resist!
Without caring any more about anyone seeing me,
I quickly collect that precious nectar from my skin
and I bring it to my entranced lips

And I savour your flavour, oh, my desire!

Chant no. 17 "The emotion of you"

Oh, my beloved!

I sing your praises
and my words soon get stuck
in my throat
for the emotion of you

As many have the misfortune
to sing of things
they can only dream about,
and long for,
without even ever meeting them,
forever,
until it feels too much,
to bear...

...but you, you exist!

And I... I know you do

Chant no. 75 "The stone and the rain"

Oh, my beloved!

They asked me
why I keep holding to my heart
the hope,
as big as a grain of sand,
that someone of your ancestry may love
someone like me

I told them
of how the dusty stone
does nothing considerable,
yet the rain deigns
to fall on it

They asked me what
rain and stone
ever gain from that

I answered that such union
makes them both shine

Oh, my beloved,
they are still laughing at me!

But you would not, I am sure…
…right, my beloved?

Chant no. 6 "Feasting on the contemplation of you"

Oh, my beloved!

They filled my cup
with inebriating nectars
But how can, those, rival
with the vertiginous peaks
and the breathtaking twists your syllogisms reach?

They tempted my loyalty
with succulent fruits from remote lands
But would, those, ever equal
your moist lips,
ruby doors to the most sumptuous temple of wisdom
ever seen?

They assaulted my resistance
with the most savoury and armoured sea fruits ,
But could, those, torment me
more than your peachy skin,
guarded by your virtue
and by my veneration
for your immaculate soul?

Yet, they found
how to break my unassailable defence,
when they foresaw my starvation

That is when, I had to accept to feed myself
with water, bread and some plants

The minimum I need,
until my soul will feast
on the contemplation of you

Chant no. 97 "Where I never went, but I always dreamt to"

Oh, my beloved!
Take me there...

...where the winds are drawn in, entrapped
into the womb of granite mountains,
and savoured, from far away

...where gypsum orbs,
from their arched pedestals,
collapse and dock, not crashing,
pulled by segmented anchors

...where slugs, hurried,
dance in circle,
and clams crave
a walk outside

...where fakir and cobra
swap souls, at once seeking
to tame and to be tamed

...where the crust is
torn to pieces and pulled away,
with gravity

...where the octopus seeks within,
talking to itself

...where ibises
inexorably peck
the ivory music box,
trying to reach the drums within

...where crippled spiders probe
lachrymose, succulent preys,
climbing on their mass,
and there sinking in,
finding volcanic brooches

...where invisible paint is smeared,
in short or long spans,
and the stringy cohesion is tested

...where oysters and sponges
learn to dance,
but then forget it
and need to start afresh

...where the lion wildly bites
the sadness-soaked clay

...where we should find the temple,
grown, not built,
and enter to pray

Take me there,
where I never went, but
I always dreamt to

Chant no. 69 "The colossus which was shattered"

Oh, my beloved!

The gargantuan feet
sink in the earth
to support the colossus
in his everlasting vigil,
but the giant
soon fell victim
of his tiredness,
and got soon covered
by a verdant sheet,
and is still asleep

Oh, my beloved,
if a perennially shattered ocean
can turn itself
into a still mountain,
could not your heart
melt its own stone
and turn into a warm sea,
to welcome me?

Chant no. 31 "Desolate stones"

Oh, my beloved!

The light prints
your feet left on the sand
are being lost,
stepped on by beasts and men,
unaware

Your inebriating perfume,
of ambergris, rose and cinnamon,
is fading, dispersed by a jealous breeze,
replaced
by smells of foods
and stinks of this swarming crowd

The sparkle
of the blackness of your eyes,
on my tired retinas,
is being slowly covered
by the dull tones of the world
my stare passes by

And even my heartbeats have changed,
as they do not invite me any more
to a joyous dance,
but they are rather resigned
to a saddened
funeral march

For my soul,
uncaring
of the fleetingness of my life,
could keep waiting for you
even when it was freed
from these aching bones,
and was meandering
among the desolate stones

Will you ever come back?

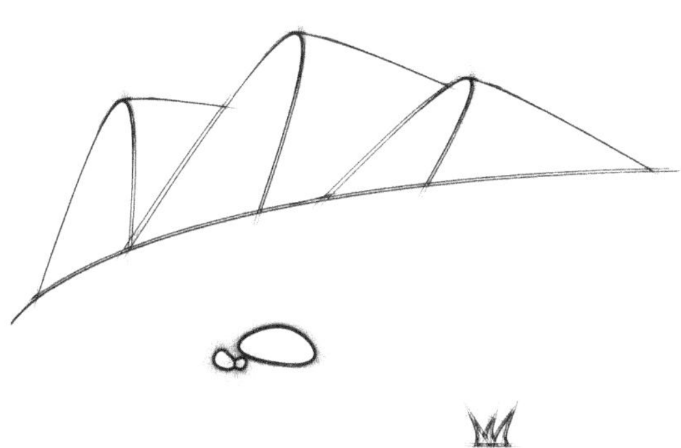

Chant no. 67 "Drop after drop"

Oh, my beloved!

Waiting for you
is like taking a poison,
drop after drop,
knowing that in that way
it can never kill you,
but only make you wish
that the torment may end

Waiting for you
is like sipping a fine wine,
drop after drop,
knowing that in that way
it can never satisfy you,
but only make you crave
for more

Chant no. 15 "Guilty"

Oh, my beloved!

My desire pushes me
on the verge
of the most sinking madness

I bite
voluptuously
the rose
that, one vision before,
I was smelling, imagining
it was your skin

The petals fall,
their perfection ruined,
and I am guilty
of depriving the world
of such pure beauty!

How can, this, be
the right way to love?

Chant no. 62 "On the steps of the temple"

Oh, my beloved!

They go, hand in hand,
chained from the eyes,
like ready to ascend
from this dust
to the unbounded blue

Sitting
on the steps of the temple,
I look at them and smile,
when I realize
that my fingers
crawl on the granite,
looking for yours,
not finding them

Someone laughs,
cherishing their own blessings

The bells of the temple play

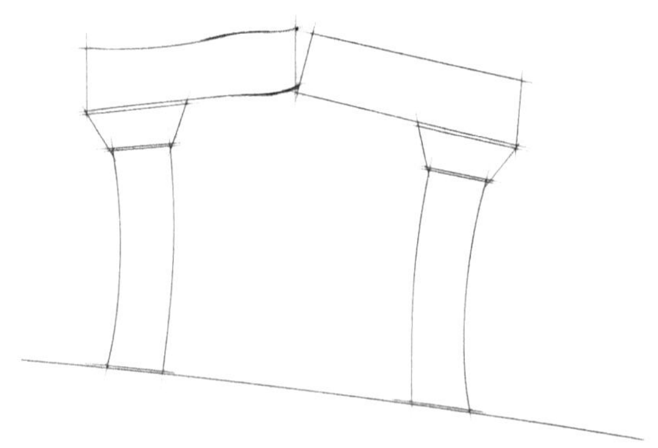

Chant no. 14 "I try to get lost"

Oh, my beloved!

I roam around,
with my desperation,
in the streets and the gardens of my town

I admit it:
I try to get lost
as much as I can,
for this fool idea I nurture
that, by getting lost enough,
perhaps, I will end somewhere else

Maybe right over there,
where you live... too far away!

But then I wonder:
what if you did the same?

Even then, we would not meet!

If only we could become stars!
...but, no: the sky is too big,
for to hope to find you!

Should we, both, dig a pit
and let ourselves fall in
to meet, finally,
in that devouring, magmatic heart
this cruel earth has?

**Chant no. 4 "You never speak or smile to me
(They say I am blessed)"**

Oh, my beloved!

Your smile lacerates
the suffocating darkness
those who hate crawl in

Your voice reaches
deep within, enlightening them,
the souls who got lost in their own agony

Your touch
shakes and crumbles
the stone trapping the hearts

Oh, my desire!

You never speak or smile to me...
Even less, you ever touch me!

They say I am blessed,
as only the most desperate ones
get to know your gift

Yet, how is it, then,
that your absence
has turned my life
into the most worrying torment?

Chant no. 58 "The journey"

Oh, my beloved!

I left the ramparts of the town,
when the Sun was still shy
on the edge of the desert

The memories of my friends' cheers,
of my father's blessings,
of my mother's laments and tears,
are, now, my only companions

I left home with many supplies,
but I was too shallow
and I exhausted them too soon;
yet, I said myself, the road to you
cannot be too long, after all,
so I kept walking,
singing songs of legendary feats

Winds, bearing sad voices
asking me to not go, never ever,
soon began to bash me,
so my rich blouse got dirtied,
its pockets filled of sand:
I dropped it,
tired to empty them

My exquisite shoes soon broke,
so I left them too, but
my feet are now scorched and bleeding:
walking is painful, now,
yet, I do it, for you

Weakened, for the thirst and the hunger,
I keep falling on my knees,
and praying, that I could keep going

I lie, who knows where, doubting this journey

Will it find me, death, lonely,
with the sole denial of your desire for me?

Please, are you on your path to me?

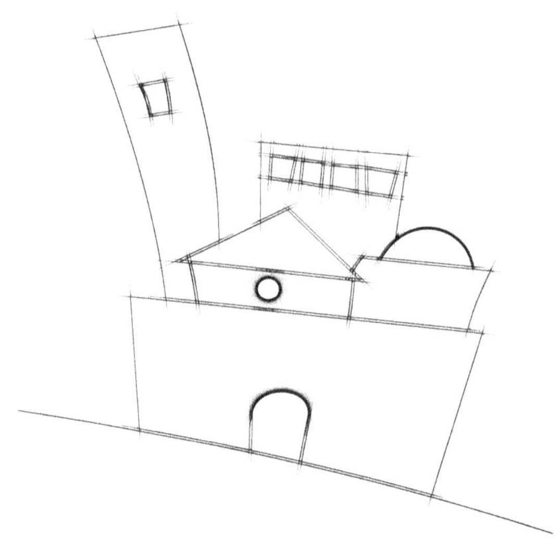

Chant no. 1 "All the water in the abysses, and just one tear"

Oh, my beloved!

I cry for you
day and night,
and my tears
fall into the sea

Honey and wine
run in your veins,
and the thought of you
is so sweet
that my tears
arise nectarous

I could drink
all the water
in the abysses,
yet nothing
would satisfy
my burning thirst
like just one tear
tasting of you

*Chant no. 118 "The hole"

Oh, my beloved!

There's a hole, in the side of the big mountain,
concealed behind a stone shaped like a sailing ship,
in a narrow valley hidden by a thick palm grove,
a hole of which nobody knows
how deep it is
and where it leads to

Say, the elders,
that it reaches
up to the womb of the mountain,
where an angel, with the wings made of salt,
sleeps and dreams,
and in his dream he listens to
everything that it is said
by whoever whispers in the hole,
and that when he will wake up, one day,
he will put a remedy to each problem,
if he will judge it is fair and sacrosanct

Oh, my beloved!

I sneak in that valley every night
and every night I spend sleepless hours whispering of you,
and of how much I desire to tell you that I love you

And I do not know whether I should hope that there,
in the dripping womb of the mountain,
there really is an angel we cannot tell when he will ever wake up,
or, rather, some human blabbermouth, hearing everything,
and who may run to you and tell you everything,
finally

Chant no. 60 "Has it started to rain?"

Oh, my beloved!

Plays, the sky, today,
with heavenly bells and rings,
loud voices of dozen towers
singing and swaying,
bent over the town,

surfacing from a choir,
coming from the crowded streets,
of chirpings and promises of twin souls
who found their wings,
one on each other's back

and these shacks and these muddy alleys
could belong to the king's palace,
or be replaced by starry abysses,
still, these lovers' eyes would not see anything,
except who is their world

I close my eyes, my beloved,
to better paint your tender smile,
and your arms longing for me,
on the uncertain canvas subtended between
my impressions, my cogitations, my dreams

Ecstatic, smiling, face to a sky and feet on a ground
whose existence I am not aware,
not any more,
I feel my cheeks wet

Has it started to rain?

IV. Delusion, Pt. I

"Because we are friends.
And I love you too much."

Chant no. 82 "The wall"

Oh, my beloved!

Your face is so perfectly harmonious
that even its imperfections
are most exquisite

Your hair is so lucent that it is believed
new stars could be observed
into its blackness

Your graceful hands should be adorned
with shining metals and precious gems,
for, certainly, they heal

Your figure expresses such proportions
that, from afar,
you are mistaken for an angel

Your feet are adored by the ground
for, when you are awake,
blessings overflow all around you

My face is marked by winds
and deeply dug by grooves of tears

My bark hair turns to ashes,
as my days fall and crumble

My hands shake, pray
and forget how to be fists

My figure, alas!,
it has always been weird

My week feet are like bound
in heavy chains

Why was I shown your portrait?!

Only our words can meet,
in a place that cannot be,
and play a joyful counterpoint,
each tongue at one side of a wall
made of what cannot be said

***Chant no. iii "By its bizarre tail"**

Oh, my beloved!

My imagination is my most unmerciful enemy!
I begged it, to desist from torturing me
with those visions of me and you,
together,
enjoying each other's closeness,
our eyes lost in an embrace
no one could ever tell

I repeated and repeated it,
again and again,
how such thing will never happen,

but it is so cruel, my imagination,
and I know it will never cease to invite me
slyly,
to lose myself in these fantasies,
as much realistic as unreal,
to illude myself into believing
that they are so much better
than this reality,
which,
in the meanwhile,
slips away from my fingers,
and I do not even try
to grab it by its bizarre tail

Chant no. 59 "Home (Among the howling rocks)"

Oh, my beloved!

I do not love you
for the way you are,
but rather
for what you stir within me

Don't you love, perhaps,
the wind,
for the way it plays
with the clothes hang out to dry,

as if it was pretending
to be one of us,
wearing them
and filling them with life?

Yet, the cheerful wind
neither loves those clothes,
nor me

It only loves
the mouth at home,
among the howling rocks,
blowing to give it life

And it is there,
and only there,
to kiss that mouth,
where it will want to return
and stay

Chant no. 89 "Regrets"

Oh, my beloved!

Should I regret
the delightful game of stares and smiles
we played for long

Staying afar, I will admit,
I, for you stand out,
and you... I would not know?

Should I regret that day,
when, suddenly, you reached for me,
and touched lightly my face
and we smiled at each other from close,
without a word,
and since then I could not help but ask myself
what we would say?

Because, after then,
you do not play any more, like before,
our distant game

I kept looking and smiling,
while you mostly looked away,
walking behind the draperies

Oh, my beloved, I do not regret what happened,
only what did not

And I still dream
of you, touching my face

Do you regret it, perhaps?

Chant no. 10 "Not even in the same page"

Oh, my beloved!

I broke the mirror
framed with olive wood
and one thousand shards insinuated
that I am not enough,
for your mesmeric eyes

I made ashes of the books
of your favourite poet
that, in vain, I tried
to learn by heart,
only for to fall at the first verse
before your compassionate eyes

And I lost everything
for the charity
I did all around the town
for to try to come up
to the purity in your heart
hinted by the golden streaks
in your warm irises

I so blame myself!
for I have not conquered your heart,
but the truth is different, and terrible!

What devours my heart
is that in the Book of Fates
my name is written
not even in the same page
adorned and graced by yours

Chant no. 46 "The cloud"

Oh, my beloved!

That frightening cloud in the sky
has been following me since I have memory

Oh, if you knew... it is such a cruel companion!
It never flooded me at once,
to throw me, from the edges of the world,
down, in the endless abyss...

Oh, in that way, it would be too easy!

It just sends down one raindrop at a time,
right on my skull

Put your finger here, if you don't believe me!
Do you feel it, this hollow?

Oh, my beloved,
I so wish I could ask you to stay with me,
as your light would certainly dissolve
that wicked rogue!

But I cannot risk
that it persecute you, too,
and that the perfect harmony
of your angelic skull
will be ruined in any way!

Alas! I have to leave,
oh, my beloved,
whose heart is like that clear sky
I will never contemplate!

*Chant no. 106 "Like light flooding the darkness"

Oh, my beloved!

I cry all day
for I long the salvation of your smile,
but you look at me and say
that I sow sadness in your soul

I spend all my possessions
to attract you with my opulence,
but you look at me and say
that my flippancy is disheartening

I forget to eat,
and the thought of you gnaws me from within,
but you look at me and ask me
who is making me hate life this much

I run after you all day,
across alleys, arcades and squares,
surrounded by looming tall houses,
but you turn to me and yell at me
that you do not deserve
such a torture!

I look at myself in an old mirror
and I have to admit that,
if I was you,
I would never think of choosing me

and this last thought
is like light
flooding the darkness

Chant no. 23 "They come for you"

Oh, my beloved!

They come for you from far away,
bowing, offering at your feet
their talent and mastery,
trying to win your heart

I hear their splendid poems
and their nightingale chant,
I see their stupendous portraits of you
and the jewels they created to adorn you

All while I,
an anonymous face among your servants,
that you don't know
and, perhaps, don't even see,
I am helping to build this gazebo
for you to spend pleasant days in

Each tree which gave these crossbeams
I whispered your name to,
every day
Each brick your feet will bless
was blended
with my tears for you

How sad!
that you will never know...

*Chant no. 107 "Like that king"

Oh, my beloved!

When you talk about me,
you have to look at the sky,
at those starred precipices,
as if the extraordinary descriptions
you paint me with
were written with threads of light
subtended between the stars

When you talk about me,
you seem to consider all the ancestries
who populated the lands
and travelled by the seas,
then your tongue, like a solemn judge,
declares I am the pinnacle of this humanity

When you talk about me,
your fingers trace in the sand
myriads of couples of intertwined hearts,
and your smile is similar to the gates of heaven,
and your eyes silently recount
of the wonders beyond those gates

And then you mention someone,

Explaining you have to go to meet this person
under the shade of the big palm tree,
and I feel like that king
who was crowned by the crowd,
and then he was left alone in the throne room,
for they all had to run
to cheer goodness knows who

Chant no. 93 "The marrow in my bones"

Oh, my beloved...

I kept waiting for you
behind the door,
to immediately open it at your arrival

I kept waiting for you for so long that...

I stopped smiling,
the lunch got cold and stale,
the musicians had to leave,
the rose petals on the floor withered,
the wine turned into vinegar,
I stopped minding days,
I stopped going out, refusing to stumble on anyone but you,
the painting in the kitchen fell, and it is still there,
I stopped letting them in, refusing to open to anyone but you,
people started shaking their head,
life has left me behind

I have been waiting for you,
but now I wonder whether you
may have been doing the same

Should I have come to search for you?
Or did you take the path?
Could we have met along the way?
But what if you never thought to look for me,
or even only to wait for me, instead?

I do not think I will be waiting for you any more
The marrow in my bones
has started to hurt

Chant no. 57 "The old pan"

Oh, my beloved!

Those children laugh at me and throw me pebbles
Stray dogs growl at my sight
and run after me in the alleys
People avoid me
and make strange signs, when I smile at them

Not you!
You are not like them!

Your gracious feet,
amber skin, perlaceous toenails,
bless the dust in the street
and play hide-and-seek,
from under the hem of your gown,
with my consumed eyes

Your hips are like hills
which shake my melancholy away!

Your blooming breasts are mysteries
never admired, always dreamed,
more than the treasure
chaining the king to his halls!

Your lips are twin petals
of tender, luscious flowers,
brewing the sweetest honey
and I, humble bee,
I imagine to approach them
like a pilgrim to a sanctuary

Your eyes are pretty fawns
hiding in the thickest of your genius,
playfully inviting me to explore it

They are pits you dig in my misery,
where I glance vast oilfields,
so that I believe, without a doubt,
that my soul belongs to a king

Oh, my beloved!

In my crumbling hovel
I covered the old pan
I once used
to look at my ugly face

I cannot stand my own sight any more!

How unworthy it is,
for it ruins the Creation
that yours, instead,
embellishes!

Chant no. 11 "You beg me (and I subside)"

Oh, my beloved!

You come to me
with an ardent fire
tormenting your pupils

Smiling with pearl teeth
as if no one else existed
or counted, but me

Calling my name
like invoking that of a saint
to implore for a miracle

Clinging to my body
like ivy to the tree
and guiding me in the shadows

And with your hands
firmly secured around mine,
excited, you beg me

to introduce you

to the person I hold closest to me
among all my friends

Is, the rumbling noise I hear,
covering your fluted voice,
that of the cavities of my heart
finally subsiding?

***Chant no. 110 "Adored creatures (Theatre)"**

Oh, my beloved!

Everything has ended

Your rite
My dream
My hope

My eyes spill tears
and it is impossible, for me, to stop them

I laugh, louder than anyone else, to fool them
To fool you, too

You already chose otherwise, after all,
for your happiness,
and you even swore:
I do not belong to it, I am not any good to you

And to let you know about me, now, likewise,
would not be any good to anyone,
other than to make me sound like
a fool,
a person who does not want to
or cannot understand

I should have told you before:
at least, now,
I would not need to repel back in my throat
each word never said,
like adored creatures
that you loaded up, until a moment before,
and that now you have to let die of starvation

Chant no. 90 "And I love you too much."

Oh, my beloved!

The musicians go wild
on drums, strings and flutes,
while the guests,
inebriated by the good wine,
laugh and dance

I sit at the table, shyly,
And my eyes dancing, on my behalf,
with your head, your smile,
your hands and feet,
and your mesmeric hips

The song breathes its last beat
and you come back
and sit close to me
and ask me, "Why don't you dance?!"

"My soul danced with you,"
I confess, in rapture
for your perfume and for your light,
"Like it always does," I add

"Oh, you are so sweet!
I could fall in love with you!" you say,
and I do not even know how I manage
to not lose consciousness
"...and why don't you?"
"Because we are friends.
And I love you too much."

And then you kiss my forehead
and go to dance some more,
all merry,
so you do not hear me say,
"Me too... way too much,"
before I drown my heart

in rivers of tears
and drops of wine

Are they all dancing,
or rather writhing like in the fire?
Is there any music, perhaps?

I only hear my heart
rumbling, desperate,
in my ears

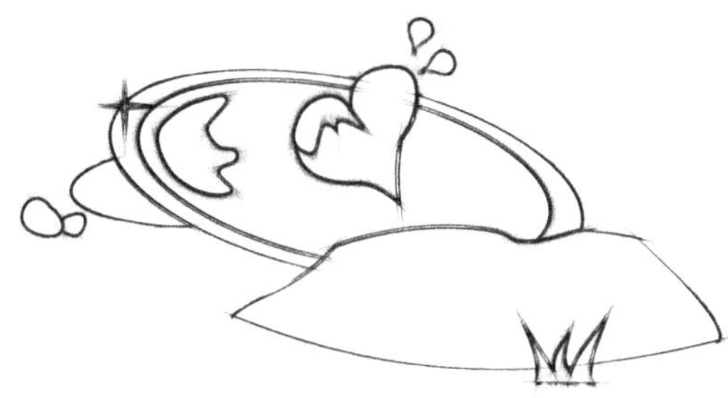

V. Beatitude

"*I ask you why you are happy,
so that I can rejoice with you
and bless its reason to be*"

Chant no. 3 "Like a miracle, when it happens"

Oh, my beloved!

I was asked
how beautiful you are
by those
who never saw you

I answered,
after long thinking,
that your beauty is greater
than that of that day
during which
the most heartfelt miracle,
one has been praying God for,
happens

***Chant no. 112 "Your smile (The fissure)"**

Oh, my beloved!

Your smile
is like a ray of Sun
rising
between two tall rocks,
hanging over a precipice
rolling down the bare side
of a fanged mountain,
separated from each other,
yet close enough,
as they are joined at the base,
like cold lovers in an embarrassed embrace

And your smile
is like that ray of Sun
when it is high enough
to peek through the crack,
more and more flooding
the shadow and the coldness
behind the rocks,
I was near to die in

And I suddenly believe,
Not just in the defeat of the deadly night
Not just in the victory of the life-giving day

But I suddenly believe
there's still hope, left, for me

This is what your smile does, for me

Chant no. 32 "I guess it is meant to be"

Oh, my beloved!

Your cheerful laughter,
your lips hastily on mine,
your fingers dancing in the air,
and then you close the door

I wander under the Sun,
among golden fields
speckled with farmers
working and singing

I reach a house:
someone works in the kitchen garden
"Still here? Go, now!"
you push me away

I roam under the clouds
following a shaken foreshore,
where mariners pull the boats aloft,
as the sea would not be forgiving

I stumble on a window:
is not, that, your beloved face?
"Again? Shoo! Shoo!"
you giggle, waving your hand

The stars look strange,
clustering like I have never seen before,
shedding a feeble light
on places I do not recognize

A warm light surrounds someone
standing at an open door
"I guess it is meant to be," you say, tenderly
pulling me in

Chant no. 50 "The most beautiful sign"

Oh, my beloved!

They mischievously ask me,
between God and you...

...whom I love the most:
I answer it is God, because
you and I exist, because of Him;

...whose command I would rather follow:
I answer it is God's, because
on His path I crossed yours;

...who loves me the most:
I answer it is God, because
He wanted me to exist, like only mothers can;

why I do not leave you for God, then:
I answer that your love
is the most beautiful sign
of His love in my life

Chant no. 41 "Details"

Oh, my beloved!

With a sigh
I vertiginously slide on
your bare skin
(and then, with much anguish, I fall from it!),
on the hyperbolic perfection
between your towering neck
and your unguarded shoulder

You sing an old song
about mermaids and the Moon,
while you comb your nightly hair

Then you let its corpus rest
on your shoulder invoking my lips,
and you observe me,
knowing I am mesmerized,
when the first hair,
like a curtain on a triumphal note,
and the others,
follow,
exponentially anxious
to trap my heartbeats
in their cascading and precipitous leap

*Chant no. 116 "Celebrate our love (People)"

Oh, my beloved!

We stomp our feet, like dancers performing
We clap our hands, like children playing

And the table shakes and jumps
And the hanging chandelier swings

We stomp our feet, like crushing grapes
We clap our hands, like catching mosquitoes

And a baby wakes up and cries out loud
And a neighbour knocks at the door

We stomp our feet, like disciplined soldiers
We clap our hands, like an euphoric audience

And the guards believe that an army is attacking the town
And the sentinels play the horns

We stomp our feet, like elephants escaping
We clap our hands, like giants fighting

And the towns in our country start to fight
And the neighbouring countries soon follow

Oh, my beloved!

We only wanted to celebrate our love!
Why do people always have to get it wrong?

Chant no. 45 "Gush"

Oh, my beloved!

I reached in the midst of the trees,
far enough away from the vain words of people,
and this water, merrily gurgling,
invites me to observe and sing

My imagination is like that leaf,
dragged away by the sight of you

My heart is like that pebble,
falling and sinking at each goodbye

My blood is like this rushing water,
when your eyes recite the verses
God composed to create your soul

And you are the river, and the spring,
the cloud and the whole sky!
And I drink your gush,
inebriated, yet never quenched

Chant no. 20 "In the garden of the Queen"

Oh, my beloved!

They ask me
why I chose just you,
one whose most regarded treasure
was lost too soon
to an ignoble scoundrel

So I sing them a song:
"In the garden of the Queen
one white rose was her joy.
But, one night, her enemy
tarnished its candid petals.

The Queen cried, and her servants said:
- Let's cut the rose,
so the Queen will not suffer! -
But she stopped them, furious:
- What is its blame,
to punish it so cruelly
and cut its life away?
Let's take care of it, instead,
so that it may blossom again! -"

Chant no. 94 "You forgot"

Oh, my beloved!

I do not know what to do any more!
Your few words sting me like thousands bees
and your frown
is like an eclipse
dooming on my existence
into the most terrible darkness!

You suddenly turned silent
and your eyes froze my feather soul!
"What have I done?!", I whispered,
shivering as if spectres haunted me!
"You forgot", you said,
refusing to tell me more,
and that's how my quest began!

I ran back home:
nothing lost along the way,
or missing, among my few things

I wrote down everything I could recall
about yesterday, but
I only know you still used to love me!

I asked my friends whether
I told them anything about you,
but they looked at me puzzled

I asked your friends, too,
about the tides of your soul,
but they laughed at me

I travelled to the northern ancient ruins
and I asked the oracle an answer:
"Shush!", is all I could get!

I travelled by the seas, but,
in the lands I reached and visited,
people could not get my question

I even flew on the Moon,
and on the rings of Saturn:
those strange folks
never heard of you

I return to you, crawling,
desperately admitting
I could not solve the mystery!

You kiss me on the mouth
and whisper,
"I find them by myself,
these lips of yours
that belong to me,
and that you forgot to offer to me,
that day,
when we met..."

Chant no. 47 "Songs"

Oh, my beloved!

Sun-scorched mariners,
their love, like a malady,
for a who knows where
you never really want to reach,
sing sea shanties
about sunken ships
still waiting to sail

Colourful birds,
who saw
mountains far away,
and cheered children
who laugh just like ours do,
fill the silence
with stories
about courage, fatigue and home

Rambunctious kids,
leaded by their teacher,
indolently learn old chants
about heroes now forgotten,
whose monuments are buried in ivy

Pious monks,
shaved heads and plumed hearts,
harmonize ancient hymns,
praying God to help them
to feel once more like kids

You
are singing that old song
that, you always say,
reminds you of me

And the whole Universe
seems to fall silent

to listen to you, astonished

Chant no. 16 "Who is the most beautiful woman"

Oh, my beloved!

They sometimes try
to maliciously extort from my tongue
words of disapproval about you,
so that they may use them to separate us

They asked me why I have not chosen this or that,
rather than you,
whether for the more gracious eyes or nose
or for the greater number of admirers

I asked them to tell me
who is the most beautiful woman
in their life
and their eyes got filled with tears
when they all
mentioned, like a celestial choir,
"My mother!"

They looked at each other,
then at me,
then, finally, at the dust on the ground,
for they understood

Chant no. 91 "I do not know (Maybe I actually do)"

Oh, my beloved!

You take the Moon between two fingers,
then you bite it and pop it,
like a turgid white grape
and its pulp and it juice roll down your chin
and down your neck
and where are they gone, now?

Then you seize the Sun,
the same way,
or at least you try, but it is too hot,
so you let it fall,
but you fear it may burn the whole night-sky,
where it does not belong,
so you step on it, like in a dance,
until it is all out

But now your feet are scorched
and you need to soothe the pain,
so you bathe them in the sea,
so far away
that you reach it in just one hop

And you notice the leviathan,
now surfacing and now diving in,
so you catch it
because you want to fry it,
but it smiles at you, and spurts water like a fountain,
so, all giggling, you set it free

And it gathers all the fish from the abysses
and they sing a mute song, for you

And you ask me what it means

And I answer that I do not know,
but I wanted you
to let the child within you out,
because I believe that is happiness

Chant no. 13 "Each day God sends on Earth"

Oh, my beloved!

They accuse me
of leaving you to your solitude
in the early morning,
and to let your eyes get filled
with flooding tears,
for to work in the market

Liars and fools!

They do not see the love I put
in conducting my business,
and my honesty
in deciding my prices,
and the smiles
I salute people with

Don't they get it?

To love you
is to do the best I can
to build the best possible world
you have to deal with
each blessed day
God sends on Earth

Chant no. 99 "Another song"

Oh, my beloved!

You sing, 'Once I lost my shadow:
it could not be found anywhere,
no one knew where it had gone
and I cried for my solitude"

You sing, "So I asked the Moon
whether it was lost in the night:
replied - Darkness is all the same,
you should better ask the Sun... -"

You sing, "The Sun giggled, and said
- My love, how could I cast
any shadow, from you, if you,
into shade, turn your flesh,
and your white bones? -"

You sing, "I replied
- Teach me how to burn,
and fly in the sky, my love,
my soul like a flying kite,
my body like a laughing child. -"

I could have sung the same song, as well,
without needing to invent a new one,
but I want them to know that
that it would not give me
the same commotion
as when you sing it yourself,
with your head on my lap

Chant no. 5 "All of my flaws (from your point of view)"

Oh, my beloved!

They told me,
badly disguising
their treacherous satisfaction,
that they asked you your opinion
about my flaws,
and that, when they left,
at the first star shining,
you were still listing

Miserable vipers!

They did not even think
about waiting and asking you
why do you still choose me

And they are not here, even now,
to listen to you
whispering it into my ear,
as long as the Moon
does not end its act

*Chant no. 102 "The reason you bless, too"

Oh, my beloved!

I hear you
sing to yourself
a merry nursery rhyme

I caress your face,
I place your hand on my heart
and I tell you I adore when you sing

Then you say that your happiness
cannot be restrained
and you begin to dance

I ask you why you are happy,
so that I can rejoice with you
and bless its reason to be,

And you finally explain to me
that my happiness for you
is that reason you bless, too

Chant no. 8 "They try to steal you"

Oh, my beloved!

Many snakes desire you,
trying to steal you, as if you were a treasure
and I, an envied wealthy merchant

So they challenge me to prove
that my love for you
is greater than theirs

They improvise before your eyes
the most glorious victories,
the most ardent poems
and the most daring oaths

It is my turn

I look at you and I say
that you are free,
and that I cannot hold you
for I venerate your heart as sacred,
and even if you left,
I would still say one day with you
provides happiness for ten years

You reach me, hastily,
and lower my head and kiss my forehead
and embrace me,
like a castaway the foreshore

Where are, those snakes, now?

*Chant no. 117 "The meeting"

Oh, my beloved!

Not even the giants
living beyond the mountains
could have covered,
with their thundering steps,
the distances,
what travellers measure
in months of travels,
what people whose mind is barred measure
in the number of bricks in a wall of rules,
that used to separate us

It seemed impossible
that everything could change in our favour,
and in fact it did not happen

But we changed ourselves enough
to decide that "impossible" is
as much true as you decide to believe it

Let me baptise your left shoulder
with my tears of pain,
until I will have poured all those
I cried far away from you

And let me baptise your right shoulder
with my tears of joy,
and then let's never forget what we learnt
and then let's smile to this embrace,
like that of the Sun and the Moon
in a late afternoon sky

Chant no. 38 "The wait (Fading warmth)"

Oh, my beloved!

Following the currents of time,
on which the whole universe floats, dragged away,
you leave the table

The soles and the toes of your feet
caress delicately the coloured tiles
composing the marine mosaic,
and leave delicate imprints of rhythm
in the silence, sprinkled with chirpings, of the afternoon

I look at your figure walk away,
your white vest caressing your ankles,
and I smile, in anticipation
of the time when you will be back,
once taken care
of some mandatory earthly matters

And I realize I smile, as well,
because a part of you still sits with me,
at this table,
around the tea, the pastries, the flowers

It is your warmth, that of your fingers,
which, just now,
were gently touching mine

Then, that warmth fades

But I still smile, with trust,
and I wait some more

My eyes venture
in the penumbra of the atrium
you entered

I wince and jump out of the chair!,
when you suddenly embrace me from behind!

You left the house from another door!

Oh, my playful beloved!

***Chant no. 123 "Spring Ode"**

Oh, my beloved!

I am like a fresh breeze
suspended in the boundless blue,
looking down
at the vast extents of the tones of your face

Not those abstract and dull
an artist would leave to the page,
but rather
traversed by light creases
and punctuated of pores,
pits, my eyes are eager
to sink in, to explore them

And each and every pore
of your concrete beauty
blossoms in my mind
like a rainbow flower

like a tree,
growing hundreds
of wild rainbow flowers

like a forest of hundreds trees,
each one growing hundreds
of wild rainbow flowers

And the skin on my fingertips burns,
in the anticipation of touching your skin,
and tickles as if it was on the verge
of growing meadows of dancing grass,

and then trees, too,
as if my guts could be wrapped and squeezed
by hardened roots smelling of soil, moss and dew,
taking my body over
to sprout and blossom from my pores, in turn

And my veins turn into branches
loaded of grapes of ripened fruits,
whose pulp is turgid of juices,
whose peel is soft like my soul
when you stare at this mesmerized me,
all shaped and beating like my heart

And these words are my humble harvest,
offered
to the altar of your blessed Spring

Chant no. 85 "Two doves"

Oh, my beloved!

Loud bells adorn their joy
with a cacophony of melodies,
solid like singing, bronzed love,
intertwined like their destinies

Our inebriated chants
remind them of the celestial abysses
their heartfelt oath disclosed,
and wish and reassure them
that each day may taste of forever,
if they will want it to

The most sublime flavours
and the most inviting fragrances
provide bliss to our bodies,
while the two doves
only seem insatiable
of the visions of delicacies
they soon will feast on

The Sun floods us
with radiant blessings,
but a cloud arrives and
showers us with a light choir

We all laugh: it is life, after all!,
and our doves are unaware,
lost, yet found, as they are,
in each other

You reach for my fingers
resting on the grass, with yours,
one, two, then all at once,
leaning on mine, cocooning them
with your delicate fire

A Moon blossoms on my face
before I look at you,
that's what I promised myself
you will always see

I gently squeeze your fingers,
and that is enough: an oath,
untold, signed by our smiles,
that, one day, our turn will come
and then the world will play
a never-ending symphony
for you and for me, as a single person

VI. Tribulations (Delusion, Pt. II)

"I do not know peace, and I crave your forgiveness"

***Chant no. 113 "As if we did not care much"**

Oh, my beloved!
Our love is like watching the sea
and its waves, coming, again and again,
stubbornly, determined to erase words
you never traced on the sand

Our love is like that sudden inspiration
taking shape, each detail crisply defined,
but you are falling asleep, so you decide
you will write it down in the morning,
but when you wake up
you only remember
how good it was

Our love is like going
to a certain place, one day, to meet someone,
and waiting forever, and raining your soul for they never come,
only for to remember, much later,
that the appointment was
neither with them, nor in that place, nor on that day
or at that time,
and that, actually, there was no appointment, at all

Our love is as
if something was always missing
and no one, but ourselves,
could do something about it,
but we don't do it

Our love is
as if we were letting it die
and we did not care much

Chant no. 19 "They tell me I cannot love you"

Oh, my beloved!

They tell me,
with a heart colder than ice
and harder than stone,

that I cannot love you
for they hold authority
over my life

But I tell them
that God's reign
is above everything,
beginning with our hearts,

and therefore,
if God wants me and you
to have our hearts beating like one,
how can they claim to have
more authority than God?

Perhaps, do they see Him
kneel in their presence,
while they sit on their own hearts,
that they neglected and let turn
into ice and stone,
forgetting they still belong to Him?

Chant no. 12 "The tree and its fruits"

Oh, my beloved!

They cruelly ask me
to choose between
themselves and you

But they threaten me
to put an end to my life,
if my choice will fall on you

How foolish!

Have you ever seen a tree
threatening its own fruits
to let them shrivel up

If they will dare to fall,
when this is just what
they are supposed to do?

Chant no. 27 "What even death needs"

Oh, my beloved!

They doubt our love,
and think we are
like actors on a stage

But this only means
there is no love that they take,
for they fear to lose it,
and there is no love that they give:

to themselves, in first place,
so they push love away,
giving themselves that pain
that they think they are avoiding

But, should we refuse to live, perhaps,
only because one day
we will leave this world?
Even death needs life,
to make some sense

Chant no. 88 "The shadow"

Oh, my beloved!

I look for you
among the colourful crowd
filling the tower square

And someone behind me says
you are at the old fountain

I reach the dragon sculpture
that since ever pours water,
but you are not there: why did they say so?

Your absence is driving me insane, now!
I hear the water gargle
that, actually, you are at the temple!

I enter the halls adorned of velvet,
I observe the people praying,
but no one of them is you!

Among the prayers, someone whispers
you can be found in the desert!

I venture among the dunes and I shout your name,
but the sand fills my throat
and my legs fail me for the fatigue

I cry over myself, for my foolishness,
as you certainly never got there,
when two hands make me stand!

Oh, my beloved!

It is you, kissing my face,
telling me you were always behind me,
giving me all those directions

You hand me
a head wear
you bought at the market,
a canteen
you refilled at the fountain,
a wooden rosary
you were given at the temple

And then you take me home

Chant no. 35 "The letter (and my courage)"

Oh, my beloved!

With trembling hands, I twist and turn
the letter I was given
on your behalf

Why
didn't you tell me everything
looking into my eyes?
Didn't you find the courage?

I cannot find, as well,
that to open it
What if I just imagined
what is most comfortable,
for me, to believe?

But, my friends come
and facetiously take it!
And break the seal!
...and the sheet, once unfolded,
turns out greedy of words

There is just one starry hair
I recognize belonging to you
And I wonder: does it mean...
...that your thoughts for me
are as many as your hair?
...or, that I am as much in your mind
as a fallen hair is on your head?

Why do you play with my poor heart?

Chant no. 18 "Questions and admissions"

Oh, my beloved!

You ask me
how much I love you
one thousand times

Every time, I answer
with any sort of comparisons and metaphors,
touching any possible field
like philosophy, mathematics,
poetry, science, and many more,
yet,
you never seem satisfied

"I do not love myself", you admit, reluctant

"So, from now on, I will not love you
to a greater extent than
that you apply to yourself",
I promise,
with the certainty
that you will understand

*Chant no. 122 "Summer Proposition"

Oh, my beloved!

The heat in our hearts burns
the sand under our feet,
until it melts into glass,
too fragile to be touched,
and then it breaks it again,
into shiny dust
the wind throws in our eyes,
rendering us like wild beasts,
blind and enraged,
one against the other

But this is not
how love is supposed to make us feel

To tear you apart,
like a ripened fruit erupting,
its pulp falling, wasted,
that's not what my heart
would ever let me do to you

So I will push the scorching Sun away,
even if my hands will turn to coal,
and I will let the night fall above us,
so that,
in that content illusion for poets
the Moon is,
a fresh breeze will caress our tormented hearts,
and we will cease to hurt within,
and we will not have any words left, to say,
but those
which are like balm for the soul

Chant no. 37 "To justify your absence"

Oh, my beloved!

It is in the questioning heart
of the night
that I revisit the day
just lost,
finding endless reasons
to justify your absence

Have you fallen in a cave
deep within the stone womb
of the old Earth?

Are you besieged
by ferocious beasts
in a rotting forest?

Are you blind
and cannot find the way,
your steps lost somewhere?

Are you persecuted, perhaps, by a cruel pain?
(So, why didn't you seek
consolation in me?)

It is so much easier,
to believe all this,
when the Sun is turned away...

Chant no. 66 "(Waiting for) Replies"

Oh, my beloved!

I write you letters
that I entrust to a merciful soul,
so that you may get them,
and the wait for your replies
pushes me on the verge of madness

I wrote that I dreamed of you:
you, of the prices at the market

I transcribed an ode I composed about you:
you, theorems of a mad mathematician

I described how I imagine our future together:
you, the decline of an ancient king

My tears blur the words with which
I am penning my darkest fear:
that you may not love me any more!

Will you give me more trivialities?

Or, will you even reply, this time?

Chant no. 72 "Easier to guess"

Oh, my beloved!

I have the privilege,
and yet, the challenging mission,
to help the people
of times now long gone
to raise their dusty voices,
from their nicked tombstones,
forgotten and lost
among the tall grass

I look at a dried sign of ink
staining a parchment,
and I wonder whether it is a snake,
or perhaps a vowel

I examine a carved sign
on a marked stone,
and I wonder whether it is a number,
or just a fortuitous incision

Oh, my beloved!

The thoughts of those people
are still clouded,
to my exhausted mind,
by the mists of oblivion

Yet, to my lachrymose eyes,
they seem easier to guess
than your fierce frowns
and your persisting silences

Chant no. 22 "Crumble and collapse"

Oh, my beloved!

The sound of your words
still shakes my ears
like a poisonous bug
stuck within, stinging and biting
its way to the brain

The thought of your graceful face
upset by a frown,
the pain from your scorn for me,
the one who loves you the most,
is like fire gnawing my marrow

I look up at the massive clouds
menacingly looming over me
and I wish they could crumble and collapse
and bury me with my guilt

I do not know peace, and I crave your forgiveness

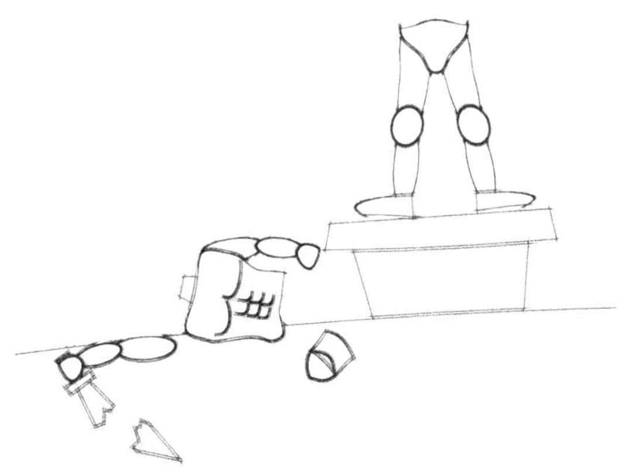

Chant no. 26 "The tree and the cloud (like me and you)"

Oh, my beloved!

My love for you
is like that person
who sew a seed in the ground
and took care of it
to make it grow and become a tall tree
and to climb it up to the top
and, from there,
to hug the sky

Your love for me
is like that cloud
which grew, black and heavy,
until it rained so much
that the roots of the plant
were torn
and the flood dragged it away

Chant no. 51 "Blinded"

Oh, my beloved!

I tell you I have eyes for you only,
but you praise the qualities
of everyone, but mine

I compose verses and songs for you,
and you wish me, shouting,
that I may bite my tongue
and choke on my mushy words

I gift you with delicate roses,
but you detach the thorns
and throw them at me

I ask you where we are supposed to meet,
and your precise directions get me lost
in the putrid shifting sands

I confess you how deeply I love you,
and you reply that your hatred for me
cannot be said enough in all the tongues of men

I ask you why you stay with me, if that's the case,
and you merrily admit that my destruction
is the only thing that can make you happy

Oh, my beloved!

I am guilty of disrespecting the name of love,
but you, your eyes blinded by your desire to ruin me,
don't you see you are drowning yourself with your own hands?

***Chant no. 105 "Your hands, and mine"**

Oh, my beloved!

Your hands have handed
the bread, the soup, the fruits
that saved many from
being devoured alive
by their own stomach

Your hands have poured
the water and the oil
that saved many from
the shame of themselves
for the mud on their skin

Your hands have imparted
caresses and blessings
that saved many from
feeling abandoned, rejected
by their own people, or even by themselves

Oh, my beloved!

My hands now, lovingly,
feed, wash, caress, bless you
to try to save your soul
imprisoned somewhere, helpless and chained,
by your mind
gone astray

Chant no. 96 "If only I could"

Oh, my beloved!

Your eyes, dry night-sky pits,
frantically twirl,
towards the infinite sky,
searching only God knows what

"My love…" you whisper,
and I, crying, yet smiling, for you,
I tell you that I am here, my love!
I am always here for you…

One tear falls down your cheek,
along a crease on your skin,
but your eyelids do not blink any more,
and your eyes do not search any more

Why is your chest still, my love?

Oh, this beloved body!,
which searched and found,
in me and in my embrace,
a shelter against your fears,
and offered to me the same,
and even more;

This body, whose passion for me
shook my heart,
blanked my mind,
turned me into fire, and led my soul
beyond the borders of the universe;

This body, which fought with me,
and for me,
supporting, supported,
is still skin, flesh, bones, and blood,
yet, all turned still

Now, more than ever, I know that
your soul - this body, being its tool -
was tide for my shore,
and shore for my tide

I cry seas below and clouds above,
at the thought of your soul, dispersed,
still longing for your body,
yet!, attracted by intransigent stars!

If only I could embrace the sky
and bite it in big mouthfuls
and collect and gather your soul,
sparkle after sparkle,
and give it a still of life,
and pour it back in your body
with a desperate kiss!

Oh, my beloved!

My forever beloved!

Chant no. 92 "Worms and trees"

Oh, my beloved!

I am in the mist raising from the fields
your paths traverse
each day

I am in the sea foam
surfacing the combers
crashing on the shore,
repeatedly, hopelessly,
at your sight

I am amongst the heads turning,
and the eyes admiring you,
when you, humbly, pass in the street

I am in the gust of a warm wind
wrapping your face
with the veil you wear

I am in each ray of Sun
that happily stumbles on you,
to turn your beauty
into a testimony
of the existence of love

I am in each raindrop
sliding down along
your cheeks,
your neck,
your breast,
like the tears you cry for me

I enter your bedroom,
while you sleep,
and I try to steal a kiss,
but I have been gone for too long,
and I do not even remember too well
how it is done

But I just could not kiss you,
anyway,
when my body

Nurtures worms and trees

VII. End

"Were not, your promises, after all,
like that smoke, that a breeze
can effortlessly disperse?"

Chant no. 52 "Interruptions"

Oh, my beloved!

Plays, the music, and we dance around,
like drops in the sea, among the crowd

Ceases, the flute, its pickle-pee,
we separate, then we turn around,
but soon, our hands joined,
we say each other "You belong to me!"

Ceases, the fiddle, its deed-a-reedle,
we depart, one more turn,
yet, like for bats in the dark,
being together again is an easy challenge

Ceases, the drum, its pump-a-rum,
laughing, we both turn around

Faded, is the music
My love, where are you?!

They dance to the silence,
turn to me,
and do "Shoosh! Shoosh!"

***Chant no. 121 "Winter Lament"**

Oh, my lost beloved!

Since after you went away,
a wind seeps through my flesh,
cutting my bones in thin foils
that crumble down into dust
other winds carry away,
to lose it in the ocean vaguely drawn in maps
they always caress and slap,
where the leviathan eats it,
and then, one day, it dies
and its immense body falls
on the ocean floor,
in the darkness, where it is lost, forgotten, forever,
rotting,
until its bones are encrusted with salt
and little creatures build on them
their houses and towers and cities,
like insane architects
defying any rule men coded,
and the dust of my bones is there,
mixed with the still sand,
immersed in that dense obscurity
that will stay, perpetually

And soon nothing will be left of me,
here above too, where the Sun still dimly shines,
but the echoes of my crackling voice invoking your name,
confused and dispersed
among a million other stories
that the wind perennially tells

Chant no. 48 "Salty regret"

Oh, my beloved!

I find no peace!
Even the Sun questions me,
accusing me of my crimes,
promising me to burn me
as a deserved punishment,
but my tongue stays still,
for I do not know what to say

The Moon welcomes me,
dressing my shaking shoulders
with its pale silk veil,
while I weep near the willow,
yet stays silent,
as if it could not
give me any hint

You smiled at me,
and called my name,
as if it was Life,
one day I could not have foreseen
in a million years

And you sipped my words,
and embroidered garments with them,
by using threads of silver and gold

And I thought that it was bliss

But now, ripped clothes
with unfinished embroideries
lie on the floor,
used as tatters,
and I cannot find you,
and when I can,
your eyes avert my stare

And I do not know whether it is my blame,
so that my tongue, my index finger, my feet
should be harshly sentenced,
or it is only a change of your heart
before which I have no choice

but that to humbly bow,
while I shed tears
of salty regret

Chant no. 70 "How could I?"

Oh, my beloved!

I have travelled far, there
where the Sun hides
and plays with different stars

And I brought you with me,
in my eyes, in my thoughts,
in my heartbeats, on my lips,
as my own token of that promise
we daringly exchanged
to meet again, one day

I saw your shoulder, your hip and your heel,
like when you take a nap in Summer,
in the outline of green hills
whose name is hard to tell

I found both flavour and fullness
of your mouth feasting on mine,
in the pulp of certain fruits,
like I never had seen before

I believed you could be this close,
beseeching my name,
in the middle of tangled forests
inhabited by strange creatures

Oh! Since when I took my way back,
I smiled for each mile between us
I bid adieu to!

And now, I will finally meet you!

I run to your door, but it is open
and your home abandoned,
ransacked!

They say,
one fine day,
you... were gone!

Where are you?
Are you lost after my tracks, perhaps?

Should I go back, once again,
and return on my own footsteps,
to recognize yours
following mine?

Or did I end up losing you,
somewhere,
for I carried you, selfishly,
in my heart, all the time?

Where could I have let you slip?

How could I,
oh, my beloved?!

Chant no. 30 "Leaf and stone (Why and why)"

Oh, my beloved!

Why?
Why cannot you stay?
Are, you, perhaps, like dead leaf,
fallen from the branch
and dragged away by the rain,
down, in that crack,
deep, among the rock,
where the water torments
and the wind frightens,
unable to do anything about it?

And after you quickly wrapped me
and made me feel how life feels,
am I, really, like dense stone,
buried in the ground?
Why cannot I come and meet you?
Why?

Chant no. 44 "Ochre, azurite and indigo"

Oh, my beloved!

Your love
is like ochre, azurite and indigo,
awesome extents of pigments
on an immense bas-relief,
once depicting a present glory
and promising
to be able to stand
the test of time
and of the unforgiving elements,

but now faded,
if not erased,
no more able to conceal
the scratched misery
of that naked stone
no one admires
or cares to dress
any more

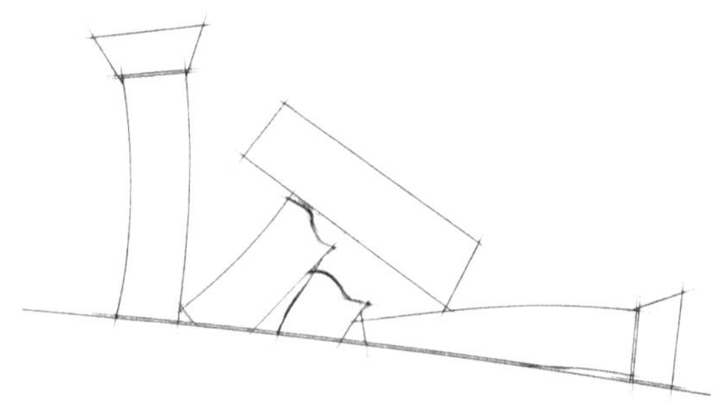

**Chant no. 7 "Why you are not mine,
why I am not yours (not any more)"**

Oh, my beloved!

They ask me why
you are not mine any more

I shake my head
and I tell them they are fools
if they think one could ever own
your skin of soft amber
your eyes revealing remote spaces
your laughter like angel's harp
your mind roaming among the stars
your heart pumping ocean and magma

Then, sneering, they ask me why
I am not yours any more

I wish I could say
I reason like I just did

But the truth is
that I wish I still was

Chant no. 53 "Distractions"

Oh, my beloved!

I run and run all day
after my duties and my dreams

I pass by your open window
to greet you,
and you sing me a song about
that angel who, all day long,
wove Time on God's behalf

I take care, all the time,
of strangers around me

I stumble on you, and I solemnly promise
I will talk to you tomorrow
and you start singing
about that mother who forgot her name
for to remember her son's

I hug my friends,
kiss mom's forehead
anywhere, any time

I walk at some distance from you:
you see, as a sign of respect!
And you sing an old chant
about that man who was invisible,
except for his beating heart

You come looking for me

And then you recite a poem about the mountains,
about their deep and massive roots

I look elsewhere for a moment,
and when I turn to you,
you are gone

I look for you everywhere,
but I cannot find you!

Where are you,
oh, my beloved?

Chant no. 34 "The sound of love"

Oh, my beloved!

I ask to the magma in the volcano,
burning me with its heat,
if you still love me, but it answers
"Groooooowl! Rummmmmmble!"
and I fear it might mean
you are furious at me

I ask to the wind,
howling so loud that it drowns out my voice,
if you will ever come back, but it answers
"Whoooooooo! Whooooooo!"
and I fear it might mean
you will never do

I ask to the sea,
whose wild waves break on me,
to deliver my message to you, but it answers
"Shhhhhhh... shhhhhhh..."
and I feel it is suggesting me
I should forget about you

I ask to my heart
feebly beating inside
what I should do, and it stubbornly says
"Thud-thud... thud-thud..."
and I think it is telling me
that I am supposed to live

just like you are doing

*Chant no. 104 "The tragedy"

Oh, my beloved no more!

At your sight,
when you mirror yourself
in a bowl of fresh water,
to make sure that
your treacherous appearance
will deceive
another innocent victim,
the precious liquid putrefies
and it becomes home
of disgusting creatures

At the mushy sound
of your false words,
even the stones
boil inside, barely capable
to not blow,
for the easiness with which
your lies deny
the essence itself
of the existing universe

At the fulfilling
of your spiteful tactics
even the shadows,
your favourite accomplices
in your lugubrious hideout,
and wherever your
poison tasting of honey
is gobbled down,

even the shadows
get disgusted by you,
to the point that they wish
to rip themselves apart
to let the light in
and expose your fraud

You fool!

Don't you know that one day
it will all revolt against you,
and you will be the one to sip
your own deadly poison?!

I still remember how it used to feel,
being drunk of that
disgusting sweetness,
and then, suddenly,
choking
on the unbearable bitterness!

I am only grateful,
for you are not by my side any more,
and I am sorry
for who took my place,
but I marvel the most,
dismayed,
at what a catastrophe it must be
being you, and, even more,
not realizing
the tragedy it is

Chant no. 21 "I will not regret it"

Oh, my beloved!

I wish
I had never let my eyes
sink in yours!

Because this fusion of hearts
is as unattainable

as the nectar poured in a cup
reserved to someone else,

as the throne of a reign
you are too low to run for,

as the baby just born and taken away
before their mother can attach them to her breast

But, no, I will not regret it!

At least, I had the merit,
of which I am proud,
to be the one who made you experience
how it feels to be loved
selflessly

Chant no. 36 "The last letter"

Oh, my beloved!

Raises, blue, uncertain
and fragile, the smoke
from your last letter
that, I, am rectifying
with the seal of fire

Were not, your promises, after all,
like that smoke, that a breeze
can effortlessly disperse?

May, then, the noble paper,
inculpable for their deceit,
be freed from the stain
of their dripping embodiment!

So that I, too, may be freed
from any oppressive sign,
written in the book of my life,
which made too hard and heavy
to turn the page

Oh, you, finally forgotten soul!

Chant no. 87 "Gifts alive"

Oh, my beloved!

You never missed, not one day,
to bestow a gift on me:
a lizard in a cage,
a butterfly in a silk handkerchief,
a fish in a bowl full of water,
a succulent in a vase

I thought you meant to say
that you too, like me,
wished
that our love, alive,
could last forever,
so I took care of everything

Yet, when you left, one day,
I wished to let all those creatures die,
like you had just done to our love,
and to my heart

But I did not do it, after all,
as I realized that your gifts
could mean, perhaps,
that life would have survived
even after the end of our love

VIII. Theorems

“Wouldn’t it be, that, solitude in disguise?”

***Chant no. 120 "My prayers to God"**

My prayers to God
begin with a thundering voice,
while I confidently ask Him
to put you on my way,
for how could I not deserve
to have you
being my happiness?

My prayers to God
go on with a moderate, and at times uncertain, tone,
while I remember to ask Him
to help me to prepare well,
for it would be awful, for you,
if I was not able to be your happiness, in return

My prayers to God
sometimes fade away among dispersed whispers
and long pauses,
while I ask Him, my heart full of shame,
how I can ever dare to ask some love for myself
when I am so flawed and unworthy!
Like a terracotta vase
that turned out to be all crooked, and hideous,
and the potter himself keeps it hidden,
for nobody would ever buy it

My prayers to God
end, rarely, with a desolate silence,
while I think I am such punishment!,
but then something, deeply within, tells me
that neither love was ever meant to be pushed away,
nor, prayers, to reject it

Chant no. 40 "Of the misinterpretation of signs"

Oh, my beloved!

How cruel, is, my destiny!
Just yesterday,
your disdainful "no!"
was falling on my neck
like sharp blade of sword

And already today,
is not, this other person,
whom I had noticed as much as a shadow,
trying to win my heart?!

But what is worse is,
no matter how resolutely
I gave no hope,
this pest promised
to never give up!

How insolent!
Is that even love?

I must leave that nuisance behind!
Nothing must slow me down!

This must be a sign, and an invitation:
you will be mine, certainly!

Chant no. 79 "Forget about myself"

Oh, my beloved!

They told me
I should forget about myself
and make of your blessed person
the vocabulary on my tongue,
the purpose in any thought of mine,
the reason of my existence,

so as to please you
and never lose you

I asked them
how it would feel,
to see your own face
replacing that of your lover,
and your own voice
coming out of their throat,
and their words
being nothing more
than feeble echoes of yours

Wouldn't it be, that,
solitude in disguise?

Chant no. 64 "One day, I disappeared"

Oh, my beloved!

I always used to say,
to anyone I would talk to,
that you were my everything
and I, just a little thing

But I wished
that I could exalt you even more,
so I started saying
that I was nothing

One day, who knows why,
I disappeared:
maybe a jesting wizard
cast a spell?

Too late, I understood,
when I saw your desperation:
how could I not imagine
you would suffer
when your everything,
to love, who loved you,
was now a loveless nothing?

Chant no. 55 "Blood of my blood, flesh of my flesh"

Oh, my beloved!

You, blood of my blood
and flesh of my flesh,
you are furious at me
like a wounded wild beast,
and hurt me back
to make me know
all the anguish
I cruelly impose upon you

I throw you
against the thorns,
in fanged waters biting and gnawing,
in the iced womb of the mountain,
into the unforgiving fire,
under the axe of the executioner,*

every time I demand
that you love
that who despises you

You, my beloved heart

Chant no. 74 "The glass jar"

Oh, my never more beloved!

After you left my life
in the most fertile silence,
I took my heart,
I observed it spurting blood
from many torn cuts
and I thought
the sole guilty was you,
with your glacial and cutting indifference

Then I put it in a glass jar,
with oil and flowers,
and I sealed it and put it away,
and I forgot about it,
...or, at least, I tried

Like the wind,
which soon will blow
to disperse the wall of sand
blocking the door,
so was, Time, for my pain

I found the jar, today,
so I opened it
and I took the heart out,
still feebly gulping,
and I inspected it from close

Like, from close,
after long time,
I relived in my mind
those acts of my tragedy,
one for each scar,

and I realized, with surprise,
that your icy fingers
never really touched it

It was me, instead,
to cruelly stab it,
every single time
it implored me to step away,
every single time
I chose you, over it

Chant no. 77 "Raging flames"

Oh, my beloved!

They say I am selfish,
and I do not know
what love really is,
for I do not hit my chest with stones
and I do not crawl at your feet,
crying
over my inadequacy

I asked them
how it would feel,
to hug a tree
engulfed by raging flames

Chant no. 63 "If they saw you come"

Oh, my beloved!

The roars and the blows
of this visceral insanity
scratch the sky, furiously,
to reveal, underneath, gnawing flames,
insane twisting of its truest and purest sense,
and dig the heart, inconclusively,
to undermine the foundations
of everything beautiful
that should rather be preserved

Where are you, my beloved?
If they saw you come,
in all of your peace, they would see
that the war is just in their hearts, and
they would wonder the whys and the wherefores

The roars and the blows are ceased,
as if they never started, as if
it was just a children play, as if
it did not hurt us all, in reality

I so believe one day you will come,
that I would still be able to hope so,
even with the world crumbling down
before my eyes!
But if you will not, then,
they will keep thinking
that they are free to pretend
that they do not hate themselves, in reality

When will you come, my beloved?

Chant no. 76 "The pearl"

Oh, my beloved!

I compared you
to a pearl of the sea,
but you laughed at me, leaving,
accusing me to ridicule you

Then, you found someone
to bow down to and adore

How could it end,
if not with your pearly preciousness
abandoned and lost,
like an insignificant pebble?

All because you have never known
your own extraordinary worth

I ask around whether they know
how I could have helped you to see,
but they are all too caught
in looking in empty mirrors

Chant no. 42 "You just do not know what it is, love!"

Oh, my beloved no more!

Today, I walk away
from our battleground
we both have
willingly soaked
with dark blood
drawn from deep within

They say "There is no sea
which does not crush a ship"
and "There is no victory
which does not leave a wound",
but I see them
surgically lacerate
their own scars,
and dig deep
to scratch their own bones,
and, in the end, pontificate
"You just do not know, what love is!"

And I wonder,
do we really respect love,
if we bedaub it
with our own bowels?

And if we let "love" rhyme with "ruin",
then, what could ever save us,
in the end?

Chant no. 71 "I have cried so many tears"

Oh, my beloved!

I have cried so many tears
that my eyes are burning
and I keep them closed
for not to see your disdain

I have cried so many tears
that on the ground around me
bushes of thorns have grown
and their fruits are poisonous

I have cried so many tears,
screamed so many supplications,
that people believe in my sanctity
and when they see me, they bow to me

I have cried so many tears
that, today, a saddened mother
brought to me her child
whose eyes are blinded by a plague

She asked, "Could you find a new love?"
I answered, "I could, but I do not want to!"

She said, "We cry and we despair for his sight,
but, no matter what we do, he cannot have it back.
Now, tell me, whose tears
are the most bitter to gulp?"

Chant no. 49 "One more kingdom"

Oh, my beloved!

I savour
the perfumed nectar
from your moist lips
besieging and conquering mine

and the closeness
of your pulpy breasts
promising to protect me
from the harshness of life

From our thrones, like monarchs,
we admire our kingdom,
this moment, gifted in fourths,
never conquered, already lost

And it is shattered, then rebuilt, again,
always intimately mutating,
and what once was white
could now be black,
or even be no more

Will our promise resist?
How can we believe a "forever"
it takes so short,
for a mortal piece of meat, to pulse,
and for another, to swear?

Oh, my beloved star, I plead you,
may want, you, to shine
for one more kingdom!

Chant no. 84 "Tattoo (There, where it really matters)"

Oh, my beloved!

They asked me why
I have not tattooed your name,
somewhere on my skin

I told them that,
just by reading it,
they would not get your essence,
and would confuse you
with many others of the same name
who are not anything like you

They insinuated
that I don't do it because
I do not trust you will stay

But I told them you are completely free,
even to erase any trace of me
from your life,
but also that you could not do that
if you knew that your name
is forever with me

Then they accused me
to be not sure about my love
and to already plan to leave you,

But I answered
that if, some day, my heart
lost the love for you, then
how could, some letters, be enough
to help find it again?

Then I left them,
to pray God
to tattoo your name dear to me
on the walls of my heart's cavities,
there where it cannot be seen,
there where it really matters,
every single day

Chant no. 43 "The best I can"

Oh, my beloved!

They pierce me
with their scornful stares,
and call me arrogant,
while they kiss the feet of their spouses
elevated to deities,
their humiliation of self
turned into conceited tenure,
for I refuse to define myself
undeserving mud, or even a nobody

Do they really consider
a handful of dirt,
or an empty jar,
gifts adequate to signify admiration?

I rather study your excellence,
to try to learn
and practice it!

You are the most perfect pearl
ever found in the womb of the sea:
I will polish myself the best I can,
so to highlight your splendour,
and give you what may honour you

Chant no. 98 "Hands (The whole firmament)"

Oh, my beloved,
who came with warm winds,
and ruffled the hair on my head,
and the thoughts inside,
where did you fly?

Oh, my beloved,
who knew all the hymns,
but taught me only laments,
who is trying to derive you, now?

Oh, my beloved,
of whose warnings I used to doubt!
You, who left without a word,
are you reading the signs?

Oh, my beloved ones now gone!
Oh, my beloved ones yet to come!

Each time I was left
with my hands all empty,
I believed my life was void,
and I, just nothing

But then, one day, I saw them,
those hands, of mine:
that's when I opened my eyes,
wherein the whole firmament
got poured
all at once

Chant no. 73 "I began to walk"

Oh, my no more beloved!

Yesterday your name
found my ear at the market,
among the swarming idle chatter
stretching from birth to death,
through the prices of goods

I was surprised, by how little was,
the stitch stinging my heart,
and by how easy it was, for the prick,
to heal itself

One day,
a while ago,
when my tears were soaking the wall
on which your portrait was hung,
an angel smelling of roses
turned me with kindness
and showed me the door,
open on the crowded street,
whispering: "It is time to go..."
And I... I began to walk

Chant no. 24 "What love is all about"

Oh, my beloved, forever beloved!

Their eyes condemn me,
right before their words do the same thing,
in the whispering shadows,
whenever they meet my smile

They would rather prefer
to see me parch and wither,
tear after tear!
Oh, they just do not know
how soaked it was, my pillow!

How miserable, they are!
Don't they believe in eternity?
Do they dare to doubt
your love for me, perhaps,
or mine for you?!

For if I let myself die
to join you,
you would suffer for me,
immensely!
"Your happiness is my happiness",
that's what love is all about

Chant no. 95 "I will let them laugh some more"

Oh, my beloved!

They laugh and say
that I spent too much time
on these books filled of formulas
that they do not understand

But if I had to comprise
our journey together

Should not I say sum up
our efforts,
insufficient if separate,
enough when combined?

Should not I subtract big amounts
from sadness and discouragement
each one of us had to feel,
because the other was living hope?

Should not I multiply,
by humongous amounts,
the gratitude each one felt
because the other was (and still is)
a living and present gift?

And I certainly should divide
weights and sorrows,
no one of us had to bear fully,
and in solitude,
because the other shared in them

And if I dug
down to the root
of what made us go on till now,
would not I find our love?

And if I had to describe you,
could not I say, perhaps,
that the more I know you,
the more you get
asymptotically similar
to an angel?

Probably they would not believe me,
if I told them that my love for you
grows exponentially, day after day,
but it is the truth

So I will let them laugh some more,
when I will say that the two of us
are turned into one
by our love,
and these are divine mathematics

*Chant no. 114 "I never thought of that, before"

Oh, my no more beloved!

We accidentally meet
on the road coasting the field of wheat
and we end talking about what used to be,
but now is no more

You say I never gifted you with a flower,
not once
I say I am sorry, but
I never thought of that, before

You say I never asked your opinion,
but I only expressed mine
I say I am sorry, but
I never thought of that, before

You say I never was gentle towards you,
but I only treated you with roughness and bad manners
I say I am sorry, but
I never thought of that, before

You say I could have valued the love you gave me,
and everything you did for me,
or, at least, what would have been better, for myself

It is like, because of some spell,
my tongue had turned to stone
I am barely able to say I am sorry, but
I never thought of that, before

Chant no. 100 "Again, from the beginning"

Oh, my beloved!

Right now,
in this precise and precious moment,
I choose to stay,
for you heart, for mine,
with all I can, am, have,

in spite of the perils and the mirages
we left behind,
which made our lungs shrivel up
and our heads turn anywhere,
but towards each other's pupils,

in spite of the inscrutable mist
we are heading to,
which will feed and grow our doubts
to the verge of our fall,
and stretch our trust to see
for how long it does not tear,

right now,
in this fleeting, and already lost, moment

And now, my beloved,
in this new, unprecedented
and infinitesimal
now,
tasting a little more
of blissful infinity,
I reaffirm all this, again,
from the beginning

IX. Silence

(Silence)

Chant no. 25 "Listen!"

Oh, my beloved!

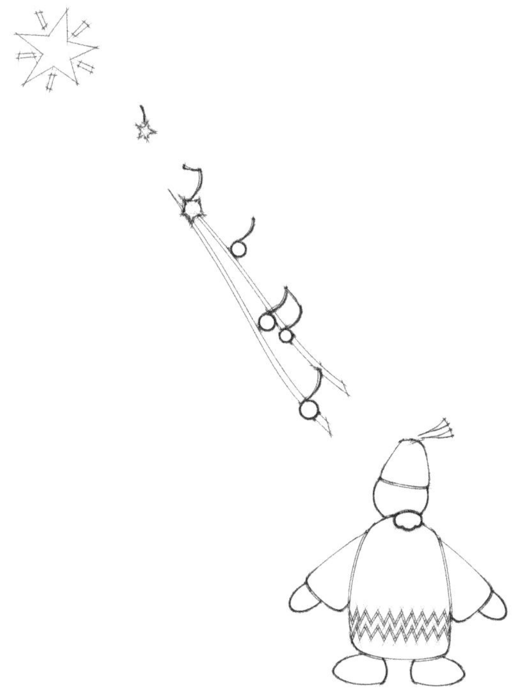

I have no words left to tell you, now,
but, perhaps, my silence,
spent to carefully listen to
your heart, your mind and your soul,
disclosing for me,
is the greatest gift
I can give you

(QUESTION AND ANSWER) POSTFACE

Q: Oh, no! More words?!
A: Well, this is a book. It's supposed to contain words. And, after all, after a little more than three hundred and fifty pages, do they make a significant difference, ten more pages? (Here I'd need a winking smiley ("emoticon") from Internet. But, given that this is a book, let's say that, after I wrote this, I winked!)

Q: Why are these poems mostly sad?
A: In an ongoing, yet hopeful, wait for a better sentimental situation, I simply wrote what I know the most: the wait... and the delusion.
But there are merry ones, as well, for which I just had to exercise the power of my imagination... I am a creative, after all!

Q: Where are the rhymes gone? And why do verses and stanzas often hold no regularity in their length?
A: Poetry doesn't necessarily require rhyming, nor a regularity in the distribution of the syllables among the verses and of the verses among the stanzas.
I am not saying that there aren't styles and genres of poetry prescribing specific rules: there actually are, indeed (even though I admit, like the insiders may have guessed, that I don't know (not yet, at least) the theory of poetry).

I am just saying that poetry, generally speaking, is about the feelings conveyed.
And I sincerely hope, with these chants, that I may have been able to deliver something to the heart of yours, of you who are reading.

Q: Why 123, and not 100?
A: Or 111, in that case! When I started writing them, I absolutely had no clue for how long I could have kept doing it, but I was almost

taking for granted that I would have stopped at a couple tens, more or less... on the achievement of the 50 chants, some of those who were following their publication on Instagram started suggesting that, well, since I had reached 50... why not 100? To make round number!

And I couldn't agree more, because, sincerely, I had had the same idea, even though I have to admit that the second fifty of chants proved itself to be, at least for the first ones, a little tougher in surfacing from my mind... probably, I suppose, for that new target (before, as I repeat, I hadn't set out any) of 100 which, from a psychological point of view, appeared a little intimidating...

But, as the Reader can note, I reached that milestone.

And this accomplishment, I suppose, other than the habit (what a ugly term!), by then strengthened, must have galvanized me enough to push me to keep writing more, not posted on Internet (in this collection, preceded by an asterisk "*").

I reached 111, the first milestone I had set out for this book... but "one chant leads to another"... and here I am, at 123, a number which, from an aesthetic/mathematical point of view, has its charms.

At least, to my eyes!

Q: Why aren't the chants sorted by ascending order?

A: I begin to answer by saying that, intuitively, the numbers of the chants show the order in which I wrote them: usually, right after finishing one, I immediately posted it on Instagram (this doesn't apply to the special ones, of course). I thought that it would be nice to keep even here that number, to give the Reader the possibility to reconstruct (and, to me, to remember it) the temporal sequence in which these poems saw the light.

The chants are not in that order because I thought to sort them so that to obtain (or, at least, I hope so) an effect of increasing intensity and involvement in respect of the content of each one.

In some cases, then, one chant is found next another because the two chants talk about a similar topic or situation, but with different outcomes.

Obviously, the Reader is more than free to read them in whichever order, for example, from no. 1 to no. 123 (or even conversely).

Or one could read them randomly, or sorted by number, in a chapter... therefore, the possibilities are unlimited!

Q: What do they mean, the chapters the chants are grouped in?

A: Like the tone and the situations in the various chants should suggest, they represent various possible phases of love.

From the wait of someone you don't know whom will be or whether and when will come (I), to the realization of being falling in love (II), for to continue with a love not yet confessed (III).

It goes on, then, with different outcomes: the love confessed but unrequited (in jargon, the infamous "friend-zone") (IV), a couple achieving their dream of love (V), another going through a lot of challenges (VI), for to continue with the feelings following the end of a love (VII)... and, in the end, a chapter including chants which try to draw lessons from the various possible situations (VIII) and a last one which, I hope, will provide further food for thought (IX).

Q: Who made the illustrations on the cover and in the book? How?

A: Me, myself and I. On computer, with a few softwares (Open Source), of vectorial drawing (that is, by manipulating primitive figures (line, circle, polygon, etc...)), of photo-retouch and a plug-in (still Open Source) simulating various pictorial effects.

I didn't make everything by hand, like the traditional artists, because a few decades have passed since my artistic experiments at school... and I think I can achieve better results in this way.

Q: What do they mean, the various symbols shown? Why do they change?

A: Once clarified the meaning of the various chapters, I think that that of the symbols is easy to infer.

The scene shown in an illustration tries to fit with the dominant concept/theme in that chapter.

For example, in the scene pertaining chapter VI, in which a couple goes through problems, the Sun and the Moon don't flutter their eyelashes at each other any more, like in the scene pertaining to the previous chapter (which represents a couple, again, but rather happy), but they rather look, each one, somewhere else... and the Moon, alas, doesn't kiss any more the Sun!

The only element which doesn't have a specific meaning, but is shared among nearly all the scenes (other than the person who is singing), is... the cat!

But I used it, here and there, to attract (hopefully, not too much) the attention of the Reader on some element added in this or that version of the illustration... and its behaviour, of course, is coherent with what's represented.

Q: But, the person who's singing, is male or female?

A: I hope I succeeded at conferring to such person an appearance (from behind) adequately generic to be thinkable both as a man and as a woman...

Q: Will more "Chants for love" come?

A: I started working to these Preface and Postface at the achievement of the first 80 chants.

Here is what I had answered back then, to this question:

"I think it's probable, provided that I can find always new situations and plots.

I have to admit that keeping track of what I've already written got harder, as much as the collection is growing..."

And here it's what I answer now, while I'm completing this book of 123 chants...

I think it's very probable, because I'm keeping writing them.

I'm at 164, in this exact moment, that is about forty more.

Considering everything, I believe it might not take me too long, to "crank out" 100 more and to publish of a second book:

Therefore, if everything will go well and if the inspirations will keep coming... yes, you'll be able to read other chants!

ABOUT THE AUTHOR

Oh, my beloved!

These words
are like strange mirrors,
made by someone
who, sometimes, dripped
blood, sweat and tears
into the molten sand
that would form the glass
you looked into

and that is why,
at times, you saw your face,
and, at times, you saw mine

but, in the first case,
I will reveal to you
something surprising
(or maybe not):
whoever you are,
we share something

Call it heart,
call it soul,
call it life:
that's it,
and so be it

Facebook: @danbergamondo
Instagram: @danbergam
Goodreads: danbergam
Pinterest: danbergam
Twitter: @danbergam
YouTube: danbergam
Zazzle: danbergam